THE GREATEST PLAYERS

SOCCER

Steve Goldsworthy
and Aaron Carr

www.av2books.com

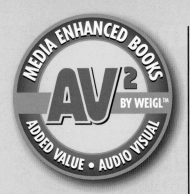

AV² provides enriched content that supplements and complements this book. Weigl's AV² books strive to create inspired learning and engage young minds in a total learning experience.

Your AV² Media Enhanced books come alive with...

Audio
Listen to sections of the book read aloud.

Key Words
Study vocabulary, and complete a matching word activity.

Video
Watch informative video clips.

Quizzes
Test your knowledge.

Embedded Weblinks
Gain additional information for research.

Slide Show
View images and captions, and prepare a presentation.

Try This!
Complete activities and hands-on experiments.

... and much, much more!

Go to **www.av2books.com**, and enter this book's unique code.

BOOK CODE

G 3 7 7 9 7 0

AV² by Weigl brings you media enhanced books that support active learning.

Published by AV² by Weigl
350 5th Avenue, 59th Floor
New York, NY 10118
Website: www.av2books.com   www.weigl.com

Library of Congress Cataloging-in-Publication Data

Goldsworthy, Steve.
 Soccer / Steve Goldsworthy and Aaron Carr.
    p. cm. -- (The greatest)
Includes bibliographical references and index.
 ISBN 978-1-61690-699-3 (hardcover : alk. paper) -- ISBN 978-1-61690-704-4 (softcover : alk. paper)
1. Soccer players--Biography--Juvenile literature. I. Carr, Aaron. II. Title.
 GV942.7.A1G65 2012
 796.334092'2--dc22
 [B]
                              2011002419

Printed in the United States of America in North Mankato, Minnesota
2 3 4 5 6 7 8 9 0 15 14 13 12 11

112011
WEP141111

Project Coordinator Aaron Carr
Art Director Terry Paulhus

Photo Credits
Every reasonable effort has been made to trace ownership and to obtain permission to reprint copyright material. The publishers would be pleased to have any errors or omissions brought to their attention so that they may be corrected in subsequent printings.

Weigl acknowledges Getty Images as its primary image supplier for this title.

Contents

What is Soccer?

Introduction

The world of professional sports has a long history of great moments. The most memorable moments often come when the sport's greatest players overcome their most challenging obstacles. For the fans, these moments come to define their favorite sport. For the players, they stand as a measuring post of success.

As the most widely played and watched professional sport in the world, soccer has a long history that is filled with great players and great moments. These moments include Diego Maradona scoring two of the best-known goals in soccer history in the same game and Cristiano Ronaldo netting 42 goals in one season. Soccer has no shortage of these moments, when the sport's brightest stars accomplished feats that ensured they would be remembered as the greatest players.

Training Camp

Soccer is played by two teams that are each allowed up to 11 players on the field at once. There is one goalkeeper and 10 outfield positions. The outfield positions are divided into **defense**, **midfield**, and **forward**. However, all outfield positions perform both defensive and offensive tasks. Not all soccer teams use the same positions. Many teams use special positions, such as attacking midfielders and sweepers.

Both teams compete to control the ball and kick it into the opposing team's goal. The team with the most goals at the end of the game wins.

Diego Maradona is one of the greatest soccer players of all time.

The Soccer Field

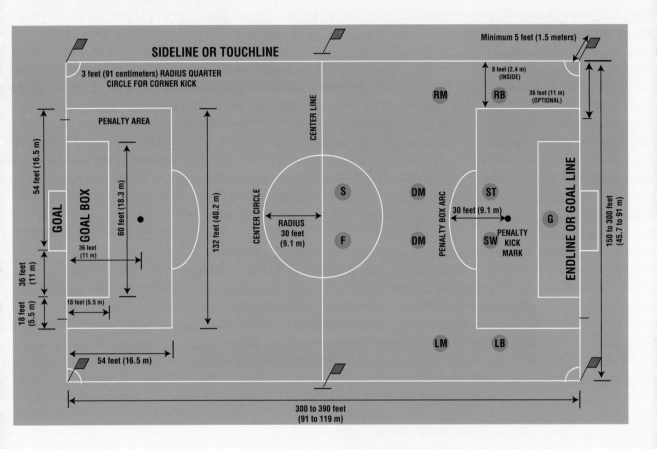

Player Positions

Forwards
CF   Center Forward
S   Striker
SS   Second Striker

> Many soccer teams use different positions in their lineup. For example, some teams will have two center forwards, while other teams will have a striker and a second striker instead. Still other teams may use four defenders and four midfielders, while others use three defenders and five midfielders.

Midfielders
RM   Right Midfielder
LM   Left Midfielder
CM   Center Midfielder
AM   Attacking Midfielder
RW   Right Winger
LW   Left Winger
DM   Defensive Midfielder

Defenders
CB   Center Fullback
RB   Right Fullback
LB   Left Fullback
SW   Sweeper
RWB   Right Wingback
LWB   Left Wingback
G   Goalkeeper

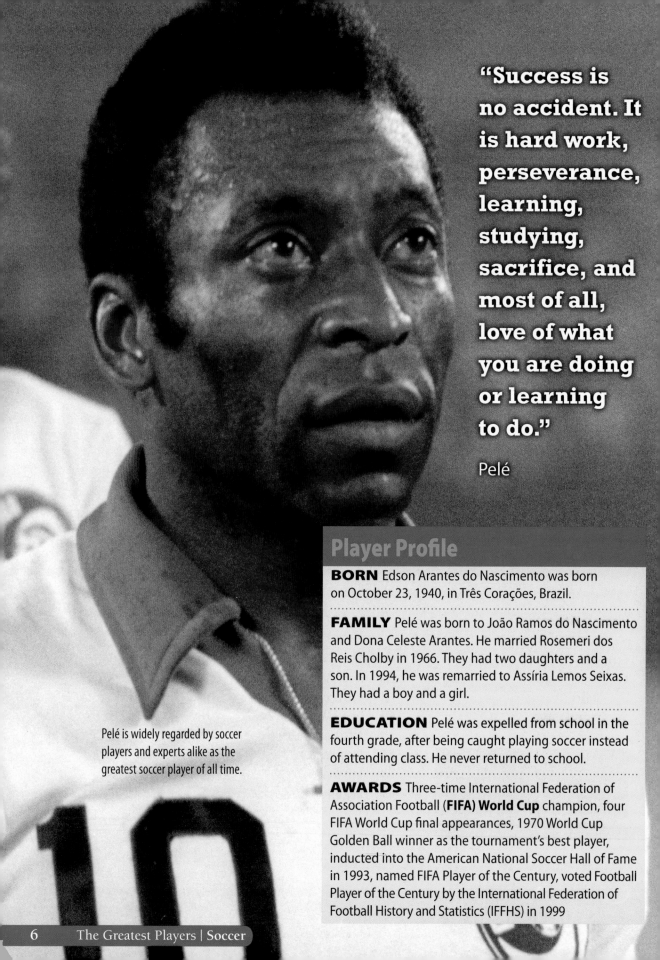

> "Success is no accident. It is hard work, perseverance, learning, studying, sacrifice, and most of all, love of what you are doing or learning to do."
>
> Pelé

Pelé is widely regarded by soccer players and experts alike as the greatest soccer player of all time.

Player Profile

BORN Edson Arantes do Nascimento was born on October 23, 1940, in Três Corações, Brazil.

FAMILY Pelé was born to João Ramos do Nascimento and Dona Celeste Arantes. He married Rosemeri dos Reis Cholby in 1966. They had two daughters and a son. In 1994, he was remarried to Assíria Lemos Seixas. They had a boy and a girl.

EDUCATION Pelé was expelled from school in the fourth grade, after being caught playing soccer instead of attending class. He never returned to school.

AWARDS Three-time International Federation of Association Football (**FIFA**) **World Cup** champion, four FIFA World Cup final appearances, 1970 World Cup Golden Ball winner as the tournament's best player, inducted into the American National Soccer Hall of Fame in 1993, named FIFA Player of the Century, voted Football Player of the Century by the International Federation of Football History and Statistics (IFFHS) in 1999

Pelé
Forward/Attacking Midfielder

Early Years

Pelé's father was a **footballer**. He taught Pelé how to play soccer. They could not afford a soccer ball, so Pelé made a ball from an old sock stuffed with newspaper and tied with string. He received the nickname Pelé from a schoolmate who heard him talking about a goalkeeper named Bilé. He mispronounced the name as Pelé.

Brazilian National Team footballer Waldemar de Brito noticed Pelé's talent. He coached Pelé on the finer details of the game. At age 15, Pelé joined the Santos Futebol Clube junior team. Brito told the team's coaches that Pelé would one day be "the greatest football player in the world." A year later, in 1957, Pelé earned a spot on the senior team.

Developing Skills

In his first season with the senior Santos Futebol Clube, Pelé was the league's top scorer. In 1958, Santos won the league championship for São Paulo. Pelé was the top scorer with 58 goals. Just a few months later, he was called up to the Brazil national team for a chance to play in the 1958 FIFA World Cup. The 17-year-old Pelé scored his first World Cup goal against Wales in the semifinals. He was the youngest person ever to score a goal in the World Cup. He scored six goals in the tournament to help his team win the World Cup. Pelé then returned to his Santos team and helped them win many national and international titles, including the Copa Libertadores, one of South America's most cherished championships.

Pelé is the top goal scorer of all time. He has 1,281 total career goals in 1,363 games. To many soccer fans, he is often referred to simply as "The King."

Pelé

Greatest Moment

In 1970, Brazil assembled what many consider to be the greatest soccer team ever. Though Pelé had first refused to play in another World Cup, he later decided to join the team. The tournament was full of excitement, with Pelé scoring six goals in the qualifying matches. During the semifinals against Uruguay, Pelé made one of his most spectacular plays. Brazil was leading 2–1 when Pelé received a **through ball** from teammate Tostão. The Uruguay goalkeeper came out to challenge Pelé. The Brazilian let the goalkeeper commit to his right and the ball rolled past him. Pelé then maneuvered around to the left and shot the ball toward the net. The shot went just wide of the far post in what would have been the goal of Pelé's career. Pelé then went on to win his third and final World Cup.

Throughout his career, many wealthy European teams offered Pelé contracts, but the Brazilian government refused to let him leave, stating he was a national treasure to the country.

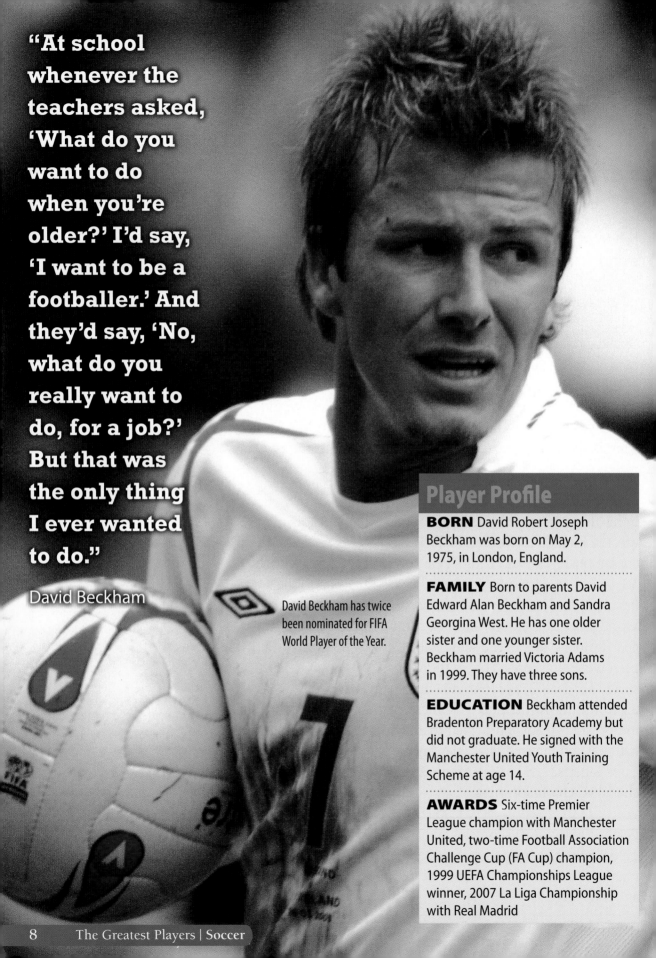

"At school whenever the teachers asked, 'What do you want to do when you're older?' I'd say, 'I want to be a footballer.' And they'd say, 'No, what do you really want to do, for a job?' But that was the only thing I ever wanted to do."

David Beckham

David Beckham has twice been nominated for FIFA World Player of the Year.

Player Profile

BORN David Robert Joseph Beckham was born on May 2, 1975, in London, England.

FAMILY Born to parents David Edward Alan Beckham and Sandra Georgina West. He has one older sister and one younger sister. Beckham married Victoria Adams in 1999. They have three sons.

EDUCATION Beckham attended Bradenton Preparatory Academy but did not graduate. He signed with the Manchester United Youth Training Scheme at age 14.

AWARDS Six-time Premier League champion with Manchester United, two-time Football Association Challenge Cup (FA Cup) champion, 1999 UEFA Championships League winner, 2007 La Liga Championship with Real Madrid

David Beckham
Midfielder

Early Years

Beckham grew up around soccer. Both of his parents were Manchester United fans, and young David grew to idolize the team. As a child, he attended a soccer school run by legendary English footballer Bobby Charlton. Based on his skills, Beckham was chosen to take part in a training session in Barcelona, Spain, where he gained valuable experience. In 1990, Beckham was named Under-15 Player of the Year while playing for the Brimsdown Rovers' Youth Team. His dream came true when he joined the Manchester United Youth Training Scheme on his 14th birthday.

Developing Skills

In 1992, Beckham got his first taste of victory when he helped the Manchester United Youth Team win the Football Association Youth Cup. Later that year, he made his professional debut as a **substitute** player with Manchester United. Over the next few years, Beckham led Manchester United to great success. He earned a reputation as a star right-side midfielder with an ability to "bend" the ball into the net. It was his power and style on the field that led Manchester United to the 1995 Premier League title and FA Cup.

Beckham led Manchester United to another five Premier League wins. In 1999, he was runner-up for European Footballer of the Year and FIFA World Player of the Year. In 2003, Beckham was sold to Spanish soccer team Real Madrid for $48.6 million. In 2007, Beckham helped Real Madrid win the La Liga Championship. That year, he signed to play for the Los Angeles Galaxy.

David Beckham

Greatest Moment

One of Beckham's greatest moments came during his fourth season with Manchester United. On August 17, 1996, Manchester United was playing a crucial game against a tough rival, Wimbledon. Manchester United was winning 2–0 when Beckham spotted an opportunity. He had the ball at center field when he looked up at the opposition's goal. Goalkeeper Neil Sullivan was standing far out of his net. David stunned the crowd, and the goalkeeper, when he took a shot from the **halfway line**. The ball rocketed over Sullivan's head and into the goal. In a 2002 poll, the goal was voted number 18 on a list of 100 Greatest Sporting Moments of all time.

In 2007, David Beckham was one of the highest paid professional athletes in the world, with combined contract and advertising deals worth more than $250 million.

> **"In Brazil, every kid starts playing street football very early. It's in our blood."**
>
> Ronaldo

Ronaldo was best known for his expert "dribbling" with the ball.

Player Profile

BORN Ronaldo Luís Nazário de Lima was born on September 22, 1976, in Itaguai, Brazil.

FAMILY He was born to Nelio Nazario de Lima, a former Portuguese footballer, and Dona Sona. He has two brothers. Ronaldo has been married twice. He has two sons and two daughters.

EDUCATION Ronaldo graduated from high school in 1992.

AWARDS Two-time FIFA World Cup Winner, 1997 UEFA Cup Winners' Cup champion, 1998 UEFA Cup champion, two-time **Ballon d'Or** winner, three-time FIFA Player of the Year, two-time member of the FIFA World Cup all-star team

Ronaldo
Striker

Early Years

As a child, Ronaldo began playing soccer in the streets of his Rio de Janeiro neighborhood. At age 12, he decided to try out for the Social Ramos Youth Club soccer team. Ronaldo later grabbed the attention of one of Brazil's best soccer players, Jairzinho. Jairzinho helped Ronaldo get a **tryout** for his own team, Cruzeiro Esporte Clube. Ronaldo's natural ability, superior ball handling skills, and great speed earned him a **contract** with his first professional soccer team. He scored 12 goals in 13 games in his first season. It did not take long for teams in Europe to notice him. Dutch soccer team PSV Eindhoven offered him a contract. Ronaldo soon became a sensation in Holland, scoring 42 goals in 46 matches.

Developing Skills

The 1996–1997 season was one of the greatest of Ronaldo's career. The powerhouse team FC Barcelona of Spain bought the Brazilian **striker** from PSV Eindhoven. That season, Ronaldo scored 47 goals in 49 games in all competitions. He was just 21 years old. He led FC Barcelona to the UEFA Cup Winners' Cup. Ronaldo scored the championship-winning goal on a penalty kick. He also won the La Liga top scorer award that year with 34 goals in 37 league matches. Ronaldo then was named FIFA World Player of the Year.

In 1997, Ronaldo joined Inter Milan of Italy. He led the team to the UEFA Cup and won the FIFA World Player of the Year for a second straight season. Over the next two years, Ronaldo was considered the greatest soccer player in the world. However, a knee injury suffered in 1999 caused him to miss many games. In 2002, he won his second FIFA World Cup with Brazil.

Ronaldo

Greatest Moment

One of Ronaldo's greatest moments came in the 2002 FIFA World Cup. Ronaldo had spent several years working his way back from injuries to join his Brazilian teammates at the World Cup. It was clear Ronaldo had found some of his former magic when he began scoring goals and helping his team win. During the tournament, Ronaldo scored against every opponent except England. In the final match against Germany, Ronaldo scored two more goals. This tied him with the legendary Pelé for most career goals scored at the World Cup by a Brazilian, with 12. Not only did Ronaldo lead Brazil to its record fifth World Cup, he also won the Golden Boot as the top scorer, with eight goals. He was runner-up for most valuable player.

In 2006, Ronaldo became the highest scoring player in FIFA World Cup history with 15 career goals at the World Cup.

"There is no harm in dreaming of becoming the world's best player. It is all about trying to be the best. I will keep working hard to achieve it."

Cristiano Ronaldo

In 2008, Cristiano Ronaldo became the first soccer player from the English Premier League to win the FIFA World Player of the Year award.

Player Profile

BORN Cristiano Ronaldo dos Santos Aveiro was born on February 5, 1985, in Madeira, Portugal.

FAMILY He was born to José Dinis Aveiro and Maria Dolores dos Santos Aveiro. He has one older brother and two older sisters. Ronaldo has one son, born in 2010.

EDUCATION Ronaldo graduated from Escola Sao Joao in Santo Antonio, Portugal.

AWARDS Three-time English Premier League champion, 2003 FA Cup winner, two-time Football League Cup winner, 2008 UEFA Champions League winner, 2008 FIFA Club World Cup championship, 2008 Ballon d'Or winner, 2008 FIFA World Player of the Year, 2009 **European Golden Shoe** winner

Cristiano Ronaldo
Forward/Winger

Early Years

Ronaldo developed a passion for soccer at an early age. From age three, he was kicking a ball around his house in Portugal. By age eight, he had joined an amateur team. When he was 10 years old, Ronaldo tried out for the **sports club** Sporting CP. Showing great speed and agility, Ronaldo scored two goals in his debut with the club. In 2003, Ronaldo played in a match between Sporting CP and English soccer club Manchester United. Ronaldo's play impressed the Manchester United players, and they urged their manager to sign the young player. At age 18, Ronaldo became the first Portuguese player ever to sign with Manchester United.

Developing Skills

During Ronaldo's first two seasons with Manchester United, he put up some impressive numbers and scored many timely goals. In the 2006–2007 season, Ronaldo scored more than 20 goals and helped Manchester United win the Premier League championship. He went on to win his second straight International Federation of Professional Footballers (FIFPro) Special Young Player of the Year award, the Professional Footballers Association (PFA) Players' Player of the Year award and the PFA Fans' Player of the Year award.

During his six years with Manchester United, Ronaldo won numerous awards, including three Premier League championships, one FA Cup, and one UEFA Championship League win. He also scored 118 total goals and 61 total assists. In 2009, Ronaldo was sold to Real Madrid for a record $132 million.

Cristiano Ronaldo

Greatest Moment

The 2008 season was filled with great moments for Ronaldo. He helped Manchester United reach the top of the Premier League when he scored his first **hat trick**. He became team captain in March and scored the only goals in a 2–0 win against Bolton. The second goal was his 33rd of the year, breaking a team scoring record. With 35 goals in 37 matches, Ronaldo won the European Golden Shoe as the top goal scorer. He ended the year with 42 goals, a record for a midfielder. He then led Manchester United to a UEFA Champions League win. Manchester United also won the Club World Cup that year, with Ronaldo winning the **Silver Ball**.

In 2009, Real Madrid bought Cristiano Ronaldo from Manchester United for a record price of more than $130 million.

> "What kind of a goalkeeper is the one who is not tormented by the goal he has allowed? He must be tormented! And if he is calm, that means the end. No matter what he had in the past, he has no future."

Lev Yashin

Lev Yashin was known as "the Black Spider" for his all black outfit and seeming ability to sprout extra arms and legs to make unbelievable saves.

Player Profile

BORN Lev Ivanovich Yashin was born on October 22, 1929, in Moscow, Russia.

FAMILY Yashin's father and mother were both factory workers.

EDUCATION Yashin left school at age 12 to work in a military factory.

AWARDS Five-time **Soviet** Top League Champion, three-time Soviet Cup Champion, 1960 UEFA European Football Championship, 1956 Olympic gold medal in soccer, 1963 European Footballer of the Year, 1963 Ballon d'Or winner, named FIFA World Keeper of the Century in 2000

Lev Yashin
Goalkeeper

Early Years

When World War II broke out in 1939, Yashin was forced to leave school and go to work in a factory. There, he joined the factory's soccer team as the goalkeeper. He knew at once that he had found his calling. While playing for the factory team, Yashin was spotted by scouts from the Dynamo Moscow youth team. He struggled during his first two years on the youth team, playing only a handful of games. When he joined the senior team, it was mainly as a back up to Alexei 'Tiger' Khomich.

Yashin's talent on the soccer pitch was soon recognized, however. His athletic style changed how the position was played. Yashin was the first goalkeeper to hit or kick the ball away instead of holding on to it. He often came far out of his net to challenge a shooter. Yashin was the first goalie to coordinate his defensive players. He also started the practice of the long **throw-in** to start an offensive rush.

Developing Skills

During his 22-year career with Dynamo Moscow, Yashin won five league championships and three Soviet Cups. He also had great success internationally. Yashin played for the Soviet national team beginning in 1954. He led the team to the 1956 Summer Olympics, where the Soviets captured the gold medal in soccer. They also won the 1960 European Championship title.

Yashin appeared in three World Cup tournaments between 1958 and 1966. In 1966, he led the Soviets to their best finish at a World Cup, finishing in fourth place. It was Yashin's performance in the 1958 World Cup, however, that showed the world his greatness. The Soviets played Brazil in a quarter-final match. Yashin made several spectacular saves, but the Soviets lost to Brazil 2-0. Brazil went on to win the World Cup. Yashin's strong play earned him a spot on the World Cup all-star team.

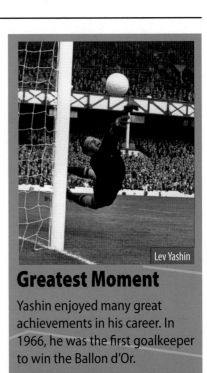

Lev Yashin

Greatest Moment

Yashin enjoyed many great achievements in his career. In 1966, he was the first goalkeeper to win the Ballon d'Or.

Some of Yashin's greatest moments came in the 1963 FA Centenary. It was a match between England and a team called "the Rest of the World XI," for which Yashin was selected as the lone goalkeeper. Yashin shocked and thrilled the Wembley Stadium crowd with some legendary saves. He went on to become the only goalkeeper ever to win the European Footballer of the Year award in 1963.

A bronze statue of Lev Yashin was erected at the Dynamo Central Stadium in honor of his great soccer career.

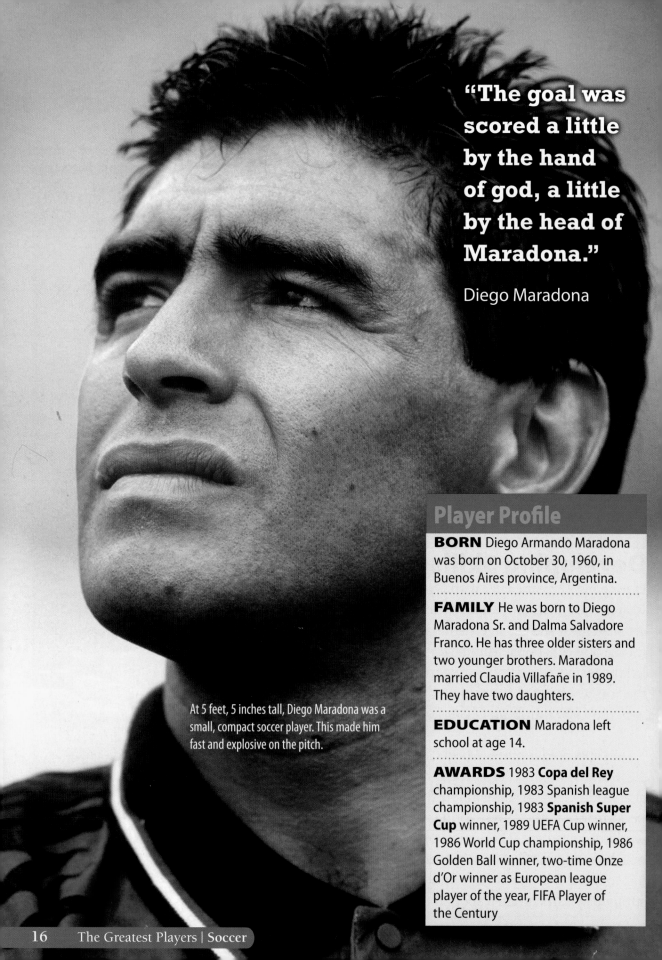

"The goal was scored a little by the hand of god, a little by the head of Maradona."

Diego Maradona

At 5 feet, 5 inches tall, Diego Maradona was a small, compact soccer player. This made him fast and explosive on the pitch.

Player Profile

BORN Diego Armando Maradona was born on October 30, 1960, in Buenos Aires province, Argentina.

FAMILY He was born to Diego Maradona Sr. and Dalma Salvadore Franco. He has three older sisters and two younger brothers. Maradona married Claudia Villafañe in 1989. They have two daughters.

EDUCATION Maradona left school at age 14.

AWARDS 1983 **Copa del Rey** championship, 1983 Spanish league championship, 1983 **Spanish Super Cup** winner, 1989 UEFA Cup winner, 1986 World Cup championship, 1986 Golden Ball winner, two-time Onze d'Or winner as European league player of the year, FIFA Player of the Century

Diego Maradona
Attacking Midfielder

Early Years

Maradona grew up playing soccer with his two younger brothers on the outskirts of Buenos Aires. He joined the neighborhood team Estrella Roja and quickly received the attention of scouts from the Buenos Aires team, Argentinos Juniors. The team put Maradona on their junior team, Los Cebollitas, or The Little Onions. By the age of 12, he was entertaining spectators during halftime of Argentinos games with his dribbling and ball juggling.

Finally, Maradona was given a spot on the Argentinos Juniors team of the Argentina First Division league. He played his first game just 10 days before his 16th birthday. Maradona quickly became one of the most valuable players on the team. In 1981, he joined the Boca Juniors. He won his first league championship with Boca that year.

Developing Skills

In 1982, after playing in his first World Cup for Argentina, Maradona joined FC Barcelona of Spain. A year later, Barcelona defeated Real Madrid to win the Copa del Rey. He also led his team to the Spanish Super Cup championship that year.

Maradona was sold to Napoli of Italy in 1984. There, he played some of the best soccer of his career. With Maradona as their star attacking midfielder, Napoli won their first **Serie A** Italian championship in 1987. They won again in 1990. Maradona also led the team to the 1987 **Coppa Italia**, the 1989 UEFA Cup, and the 1990 Italian Super Cup.

Diego Maradona

Greatest Moment

Maradona's greatest moment came in the 1986 World Cup. During the quarter-final against England, he scored two of the best-known goals in soccer history. Maradona scored his first goal by punching the ball into the net. The goal should not have counted because of the **hand ball**, but the referee did not see it. The goal later became known later as "the hand of God." However, Maradona's second goal was one for the history books. He carried the ball half the length of the field, turning past five English defenders and past the goalkeeper before scoring. Argentina won the game 2–1 and went on to win the World Cup. The goal was later voted the "Goal of the Century."

Diego Maradona is the only player to win the Golden Ball at both the FIFA Under-20 World Cup and the FIFA World Cup.

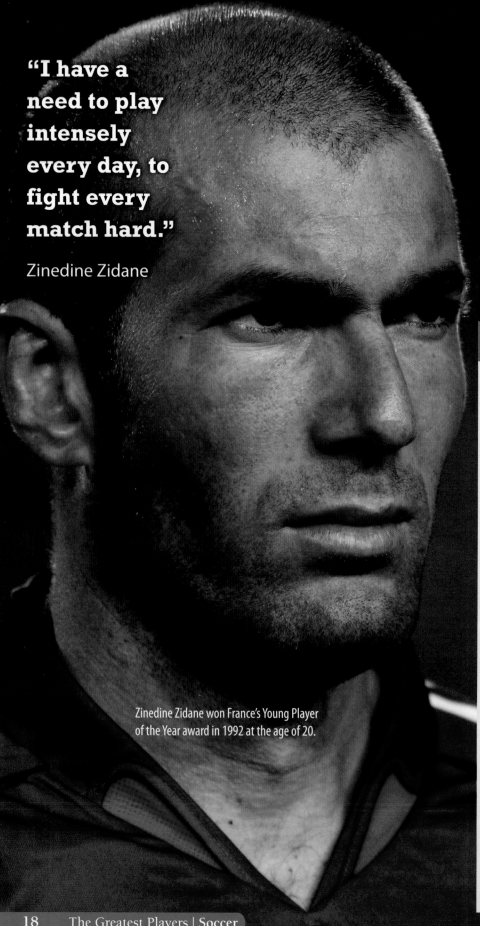

"I have a need to play intensely every day, to fight every match hard."

Zinedine Zidane

Zinedine Zidane won France's Young Player of the Year award in 1992 at the age of 20.

Player Profile

BORN Zinedine Yazid Zidane was born on June 23, 1972, in Marseilles, France.

FAMILY He was born to Algerian immigrants Smail and Malika Zidane. He has three brothers and a sister. Zidane is married to Véronique Fernandéz. They have four sons.

EDUCATION He left school at age 14 to pursue a career in soccer.

AWARDS 1998 FIFA World Cup champion, two-time Serie A champion, 1997 Italian Super Cup champion, two-time UEFA Super Cup champion, two-time Intercontinental Cup winner, 2002 UEFA Champions League champion, 1998 Ballon d'Or winner, three-time Onze d'Or winner, three-time FIFA World Player of the Year, 2006 FIFA World Cup Golden Ball winner

Zinedine Zidane
Attacking Midfielder

Early Years

Zidane's childhood was filled with soccer. Growing up in Marseille, Zidane avoided the trouble some neighborhood kids fell into by devoting himself to soccer. By age 12, he was playing with a local team. Two years later, he joined a junior team in Cannes. Scout Jean Varraud was so impressed by the young player, he offered him a tryout. Zidane later signed a contract to play for AS Cannes of the French league.

In 1992, Zidane moved to the top French league division with Girondins de Bordeaux. He helped the club win the 1995 **Intertoto Cup**. The next season, he joined the Italian league with Juventus of Turin. He won five championships with Juventus, including two Serie A wins, one Italian Super Cup and one UEFA Super Cup.

Developing Skills

In 2001, Zidane signed with powerhouse soccer club Real Madrid of the Spanish league. His teammates included soccer greats Ronaldo and David Beckham. Zidane continued to shine. In 2002, Real Madrid won the 2002 UEFA Champions League final on a sensational game-winning goal by Zidane. The goal was even more impressive because Zidane scored it with his left foot, which is not his usual striking foot.

In 2003, Zidane and his teammates captured the La Liga championship. He also won his third FIFA World Player of the Year award that season. Only one other person has ever won the award three times, his Real Madrid teammate Ronaldo. In 2004, UEFA fans voted Zidane the best footballer of the previous 50 years.

Zinedine Zidane

Greatest Moment

Some of Zidane's greatest moments came in international play. He was often at his best at the FIFA World Cup.

The 1998 World Cup was held in France. Zidane and the French team faced the favored Brazilian team in the final. Zidane scored two goals from **headers**, and France went on to win the match 3–0. It was the first ever World Cup championship for France. Zidane was named Man of the Match for the World Cup Final.

Zinedine Zidane was awarded the Golden Ball as best player of the 2006 FIFA World Cup despite being sent off in the final for headbutting an opposing player.

> **"You have got to shoot, otherwise you can't score."**
>
> Johan Cruyff

Johan Cruyff was famous for developing a move called "the Cruyff turn" at the 1974 FIFA World Cup.

Player Profile

BORN Hendrik Johannes Cruyff was born on April 25, 1947, in Amsterdam, Netherlands.

FAMILY Cruyff's mother was a laundry woman at the Ajax football stadium. His father died of a heart attack when Cruyff was 12 years old. Cruyff married Danny Coster in 1968. They have two daughters and a son.

EDUCATION Cruyff left school at age 13 to pursue a career in soccer.

AWARDS Three-time European Cup champion, two-time UEFA Super Cup champion, 1974 La Liga champion, 1978 Copa del Rey champion, four-time Dutch Footballer of the Year, 1974 Golden Ball winner, three-time Ballon d'Or winner

Johan Cruyff
Attacking Midfielder

Early Years

From an early age, Cruyff had a natural ability in soccer. At age 10, he joined the Ajax youth system. For seven years, he worked hard to improve his game. Finally, he moved up to the senior Ajax team in 1964. Two years later, Cruyff scored 25 goals in 23 games and led his team to a league championship. They repeated the win in 1967 and also took home the **Dutch Cup**. Cruyff was the leading goal scorer in the league with 33 goals that year. In 1968, Ajax won another league championship, and Cruyff was named Dutch Footballer of the Year. In his nine years with Ajax, Cruyff won three European Cups, five Dutch Cups, two UEFA Super Cups, and one Intercontinental Cup. Cruyff was sold to FC Barcelona in the summer of 1973.

Developing Skills

In many ways, Cruyff's greatness is measured not so much by his championships, but by how his style of play changed the game. With Ajax coach Rinus Michels, Cruyff developed a style of soccer known as "Total Football." Instead of playing one position the whole game, Cruyff would "float" into a winger or defender position, as would all the other players on his team. This created a revolutionary style of play that was both fluid and effective.

Cruyff used this style in the 1974 World Cup tournament. Team Netherlands won its first three matches without giving up a single goal. In the opening minutes of the final against West Germany, Cruyff and his teammates controlled the ball with 13 touches before scoring a goal. The Germans had not touched the ball once. Though the Netherlands lost the tournament, Cruyff's style changed the game of soccer forever.

Johan Cruyff

Greatest Moment

Cruyff had many great moments during his career. His appearance at the 1974 FIFA World Cup was full of great moments.

One of the greatest moments for Cruyff came during his play with FC Barcelona, when he scored what would become known as "the phantom goal." Barcelona was playing a game against Atlético Madrid, and Cruyff was on the field. His teammates took the ball down the field, kicking it toward the net at neck height. It sailed past the far post when Cruyff seemed to appear from nowhere, leapt into the air, twisted away from the net, and extended his foot to "karate-kick" the ball into the goal with his heel.

In 1999, Johan Cruyff was voted European Player of the Century by the International Federation of Football History and Statistics. FIFA later named him runner-up to Pelé as World Player of the Century.

> "It is not the strong one that wins, the one that wins is strong."

Franz Beckenbauer

Franz Beckenbauer was nicknamed *Der Kaiser*, which means "The King" or "The Emperor," for his elegant style and mastery on the soccer field.

Player Profile

BORN Franz Anton Beckenbauer was born on September 11, 1945, in Munich, Germany.

FAMILY Beckenbauer was born to Franz Beckenbauer Sr. and Antonie Beckenbauer. He has been married three times and has five children.

EDUCATION He left school at age 15.

AWARDS 1974 FIFA World Cup champion, 1990 FIFA World Cup champion as a coach, three-time European Cup champion, 1967 UEFA Cup Winners' Cup champion, 1972 UEFA European Football Championship winner, two-time Ballon d'Or winner, four-time German Footballer of the Year

Franz Beckenbauer

Sweeper

Early Years

Beckenbauer grew up in Munich idolizing German soccer great Fritz Walter and dreaming of one day playing the sport himself. In 1958, at the age of 13, Beckenbauer joined the FC Bayern Munich youth team, playing center forward. In 1964, Beckenbauer moved up to the senior team as a left winger. The team soon gained success in the new German league, winning the German Cup and the European Cup Winners' Cup in 1967. Beckenbauer was named captain of the team in 1968 and led Bayern Munich to its first league title. The team went on to win three league championships and three European Cups. During his time with Bayern Munich, Beckenbauer became one of the most celebrated and decorated soccer players in the history of the game.

Developing Skills

Shortly after becoming the captain at Bayern Munich, Beckenbauer switched his position to defense. It was at this time that he developed a defensive role of *libero*, or sweeper. Beckenbauer could often anticipate an attack before it developed. He challenged opposing forwards and swept the ball away from them. He then either started a counter-attack, or took the ball downfield for a shot on goal.

Beckenbauer used these techniques to wow crowds at three World Cup tournaments. At the 1970 World Cup, West Germany faced Italy in a semifinal match that has been called the "Game of the Century." The game ended in a 4–3 loss for West Germany, but Beckenbauer played a great game, despite having fractured his collarbone earlier in the match.

Franz Beckenbauer

Greatest Moment

Considered by most to be the greatest German soccer player of all time, Beckenbauer has experienced many great moments. In 1999, the IFFHS voted him second place behind Johan Cruyff as the European Player of the Century, and third place behind Pelé and Cruyff as World Player of the Century.

In 1974, Beckenbauer captained the German team at the FIFA World Cup. The final saw Beckenbauer and his "sweeper" position battle Johan Cruyff of the Netherlands and his "Total Football" technique. The result was a thrilling match that saw Beckenbauer and his German team hoist the World Cup as champions. Germany was the only national team at the time to hold both the World Cup and the European Cup at the same time.

Franz Beckenbauer is the only soccer player to win the FIFA World Cup as both a player and a coach.

"I will write of my life as a footballer as if it were a love story, for who shall say that it is not?"

Ferenc Puskás

Ferenc Puskás was one of the greatest all-time scorers in soccer, with an amazing 1,176 career goals.

Player Profile

BORN Ferenc Purczeld was born on April 2, 1927, in Budapest, Hungary.

FAMILY Puskás' father, Ferenc Sr., was a soccer player and coach. He changed the family name to Puskás when his son was 10 years old. Puskás married Erzsébet in 1949. They had one daughter.

EDUCATION Puskás left school at age 12 to pursue a career in soccer.

AWARDS Five-time La Liga champion, three-time European Cup champion, 1960 Intercontinental Cup champion, 1952 Olympic gold medal in soccer, 1953 Central European champion, 1953 World Soccer Player of the Year, 1953 European Player of the Year

Ferenc Puskás
Forward

Early Years

Puskás' father was a soccer coach in Kispest, Hungary. He encouraged his son to pursue a career in soccer. Young Puskás was a natural. By age 10, he was playing for the local Kispest club. In 1943, he played his first match as a member of the senior Kispest team. The team became Budapest Honvéd in 1949. Puskás helped the team win the Hungarian league title five times. He was the league's top scorer four times.

In 1945, Puskás made his debut with the Hungarian national team, also known as the Mighty Magyars. During his time with the national team, Puskás scored 84 goals in 85 matches. He also led the national team to an Olympic gold medal and a Central European Championship.

Developing Skills

When armed conflict erupted in Hungary in 1956, Puskás left his homeland in search of a new team. At 30 years of age, many thought his best years had passed. However, Real Madrid of Spain decided to take a chance on the legendary player.

Puskás proved to Real Madrid and the world that he was far from done with soccer. He scored four hat tricks during his first La Liga season. In fact, in his eight years with Real Madrid, Puskás scored a total of 157 goals in 182 games. Several of these games were multi-goal games for Puskás. With Puskás on a team that included soccer legend Alfredo Di Stéfano, Real Madrid won five straight La Liga championships from 1960 to 1965. The team also won three European Cups.

Ference Puskás

Greatest Moment

Puskás has enjoyed many great moments in soccer. In the 1960 European Cup final match against Eintracht Frankfurt, Puskás scored four goals to help his team win 7–3. The game is widely considered one of the greatest matches ever played.

While with Hungary's national team, Puskás and his teammates went on an unbelievable winning streak of 32 games. It was during this run that they went to the 1952 Olympics. The Mighty Magyar dominated the event. Puskás seemed unstoppable. He recorded four goals, including the game-winner in the final, to capture the gold medal.

In 2009, FIFA introduced the FIFA Puskás Award to the soccer player who had scored the "most beautiful" goal that season.

Greatest Moments

1966 – Goal or No Goal?

When: July 30, 1966

Where: London, England

The World Cup final between England and West Germany ended in a 2–2 draw after regulation time. In extra time, Geoff Hurst of England took a shot on the West German goal. The ball hit the crossbar and bounced straight down. The West German goalkeeper then cleared the ball, but the referees called it a goal. West Germany denied that the ball had crossed the line, but the goal stood. England won the game 4–2.

1960
Ferenc Puskás scores four goals to lead Real Madrid to a European Cup victory.

1974
Johan Cruyff scores his "phantom goal" for FC Barcelona.

1940   **1950**   **1960**   **1970**   **1980**

1986 – The Hand of God

When: June 22, 1986

Where: Mexico City, Mexico

In the World Cup quarter-final between Argentina and England, Diego Maradona scored the most controversial goal in soccer history. The goal is known as "The Hand of God" because Maradona directed it into the net with his hand. The referee thought Maradona used his head to knock the ball into the net, and the goal stood. Argentina won the match 2–1.

1966
Lev Yashin becomes the first goalkeeper to win the Ballon d'Or.

1970
Pelé wins his third World Cup.

1996
David Beckham scores a goal from the halfway line to help Manchester United defeat Wimbledon.

2002 – Zidane's Volley

When: May 15, 2002

Where: Glasgow, Scotland

When Real Madrid and Leverkusen squared off in the European Cup championship game, Madrid was considered the heavy favorite. Madrid opened the scoring in the eighth minute, but Leverkusen tied it up just five minutes later. The game stayed deadlocked until the 45th minute, when Zinedine Zidane scored what many think to be one of the best goals in Champions League history. Zidane took a high, arching cross pass on the edge of the penalty area. Without hesitating, Zidane **volleyed** the ball with his left foot into the top corner of the net. Real Madrid won the championship 2–1.

2002
Ronaldo scores his 12th career World Cup goal, tying a previous record set by Pelé.

2008
Cristiano Ronaldo scores 42 goals in a season to set a record for midfielders.

| 1990 | 2000 | 2005 | 2010 | 2015 |

1998
Zinedine Zidane scores twice in France's World Cup victory over Brazil.

1999
Franz Beckenbauer is named one of the greatest players of the century.

2004 – The Invincibles

When: 2003–2004 English Premier League season

Where: London, England

The 2003–2004 Arsenal soccer team was one of the greatest teams to take the field in the history of the English Premier League. That season, Arsenal went unbeaten through all 38 league matches, posting a record of 26 wins, 12 draws, and no losses. The team's undefeated run would eventually extend to 49 games, which set a new league record. In all, Arsenal won 36 games, drew 13, and lost none. Upon winning the English Premiership at the end of the season, the league had a special gold version of the league title to celebrate the team that is now known as "The Invincibles."

27

Write a Biography

Life Story

A person's life story can be the subject of a book. This kind of book is called a biography. Biographies often describe the lives of people who have achieved great success. These people may be alive today, or they may have lived many years ago. Reading a biography can help you learn more about a great person.

Get the Facts

Use this book, and research in the library and on the Internet, to find out more about your favorite soccer player. Learn as much about this player as you can. What team did this person play for? What are his or her statistics in important categories? Has this person set any records? Be sure to also write down key events in the person's life. What was this person's childhood like? What has he or she accomplished? Is there anything else that makes this person special or unusual?

Use the Concept Web

A concept web is a useful research tool. Read the questions in the concept web on the following page. Answer the questions in your notebook. You answers will help you write a biography.

Cristiano Ronaldo wears number 7 on his jersey for Real Madrid. Many soccer teams give this number to their best player.

Concept Web

- Where does this individual currently reside?
- Does he or she have a family?

- What did you learn from the books you read in your research?
- Would you suggest these books to others?
- Was anything missing from these books?

- Where and when was this person born?
- Describe his or her parents, siblings, and friends.
- Did this person grow up in unusual circumstances?

Your Opinion

Adulthood

Childhood

WRITING A BIOGRAPHY

Main Accomplishments

Help and Obstacles

Work and Preparation

- What is this person's life's work?
- Has he or she received awards or recognition for accomplishments?
- How have this person's accomplishments served others?

- What was this person's education?
- What was his or her work experience?
- How does this person work; what is the process he or she uses?

- Did this individual have a positive attitude?
- Did he or she receive help from others?
- Did this person have a mentor?
- Did this person face any hardships?
- If so, how were the hardships overcome?

29

Know your STUFF!

1 Who is the top goal scorer of all time?

2 Who scored a goal from the halfway line?

3 Which of Pelé's records did Ronaldo tie in the 2002 World Cup?

4 Which midfielder set a record of 42 goals in one season?

5 Who was the first goalkeeper to win the Ballon d'Or?

6 What is Diego Maradona best remembered for?

7 Who are the only players to win the FIFA World Player of the Year award three times?

8 What is Johan Cruyff best known for?

9 Who is considered the greatest German soccer player of all time?

10 Who led Real Madrid to five straight La Liga championships in the 1960s?

Glossary

Ballon d'Or: an award given to the European player of the year from 1956 to 2009; in 2010, it became the FIFA Ballon d'Or for world player of the year

contract: a written agreement to play for a team

Copa del Rey: annual championship competition for the top soccer teams in Spain

Coppa Italia: annual championship competition for the top soccer teams in Italy

defense: players who try to keep the other team from scoring

Dutch Cup: annual championship competition for the top soccer teams in the Netherlands

European Golden Shoe: award given each year to the player who scores the most goals in Europe's top soccer leagues

FIFA: the governing organization that oversees international competition for soccer; "FIFA" comes from the French name *Fédération Internationale de Football Association*

footballer: a person who plays soccer

forward: a player who tries to score goal against his or her opponent

halfway line: a line that runs across the middle of a soccer field

hand ball: a foul called in soccer for touching the ball with a hand

hat trick: scoring three goals in one game

headers: goals scored by directing the ball into the net using the head

Intertoto Cup: a championship for European teams from 1961 to 2008

midfield: players positioned between the forwards and defense who share both offensive and defensive duties

Serie A: the top professional soccer league in Italy

Silver Ball: award given to the player judged to be second best in the World Cup final

Soviet: former name for a group of countries in Eastern Europe

Spanish Super Cup: a championship played between the winners of Spain's top two soccer competitions

sports club: an organization that fields teams in many sports across multiple age groups and skill levels

striker: a soccer player who focuses mainly on scoring goals

substitute: a backup player who replaces another player on the field

through ball: a pass that travels through defenders before reaching its target

throw-in: a play where a soccer ball is thrown back into play after it has left the field

tryout: perform to try to join a team

volleyed: kicked the ball out of mid air

World Cup: a championship competition held every four years between the best national soccer teams in the world

Index

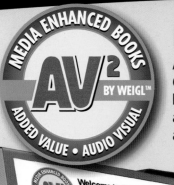

Log on to www.av2books.com

AV² by Weigl brings you media enhanced books that support active learning. Go to www.av2books.com, and enter the special code found on page 2 of this book. You will gain access to enriched and enhanced content that supplements and complements this book. Content includes video, audio, web links, quizzes, a slide show, and activities.

Audio
Listen to sections of the book read aloud.

Video
Watch informative video clips.

Embedded Weblinks
Gain additional information for research.

Try This!
Complete activities and hands-on experiments.

WHAT'S ONLINE?

Try This!	Embedded Weblinks	Video	EXTRA FEATURES
Try a soccer activity.	Learn more about soccer players.	Watch a video about soccer.	
Test your knowledge of soccer equipment.	Read about soccer coaches.	View stars of the sport in action.	
Complete a mapping activity.	Find out more about where soccer games take place.	Watch a video about soccer players.	

Audio
Listen to sections of the book read aloud.

Key Words
Study vocabulary, and complete a matching word activity.

Slide Show
View images and captions, and prepare a presentation.

Quizzes
Test your knowledge.

AV² was built to bridge the gap between print and digital. We encourage you to tell us what you like and what you want to see in the future.

Sign up to be an AV² Ambassador at www.av2books.com/ambassador.